AFGHANISTAN 2016 HUMAN RIGHTS REPORT

EXECUTIVE SUMMARY

Afghanistan is an Islamic Republic with a directly elected president, a bicameral legislative branch, and a judicial branch. Based on the electoral calendar specified in the constitution, parliamentary elections should have taken place in 2015; however, they did not take place in either 2015 or 2016.

Civilian authorities generally maintained control over the security forces, although there were occasions when security forces acted independently.

The most significant human rights problems were widespread violence, including indiscriminate attacks on civilians by armed insurgent groups; armed insurgent groups' killings of persons affiliated with the government; torture and abuse of detainees by government forces; widespread disregard for the rule of law and little accountability for those who committed human rights abuses; and targeted violence and endemic societal discrimination against women and girls.

Other human rights problems included extrajudicial killings by security forces; ineffective government investigations of abuse and torture by local security forces; poor prison conditions; arbitrary arrest and detention, including of women accused of so-called moral crimes; prolonged pretrial detentions; judicial corruption and ineffectiveness; violations of privacy rights; restrictions on freedom of speech, press, religion, and movement; pervasive governmental corruption; underage and forced marriages; abuse of children, including sexual abuse; trafficking in persons, including forced labor; discrimination against persons with disabilities; discrimination and abuses against ethnic minorities; societal discrimination based on race, religion, gender, sexual orientation, and HIV/AIDS status; and abuse of workers' rights, including child labor.

Widespread disregard for the rule of law and official impunity for those who committed human rights abuses were serious problems. The government did not consistently or effectively prosecute abuses by officials, including security forces.

The Taliban and other insurgents continued to kill security force personnel and civilians, including journalists, using indiscriminate tactics such as improvised explosive devices (IEDs), car bombs, suicide attacks, rocket attacks, and armed attacks. The UN Assistance Mission in Afghanistan (UNAMA) attributed 61 percent of civilian casualties (1,569 deaths and 3,574 injured) to nonstate actors.

The Taliban used children as suicide bombers, soldiers, and weapons carriers. Other antigovernment elements threatened, robbed, kidnapped, and attacked villagers, foreigners, civil servants, and medical and nongovernmental organization (NGO) workers. Authorities did not effectively investigate or prosecute most of these abuses.

Section 1. Respect for the Integrity of the Person, Including Freedom from:

a. Arbitrary Deprivation of Life and other Unlawful Politically Motivated Killings

There were credible reports the government or its agents committed arbitrary or unlawful killings. For example, in February UNAMA received a report of Afghan Local Police (ALP) members detaining, torturing, and executing a shepherd after an IED killed two ALP members.

NGOs, UNAMA, and media throughout the year charged progovernment forces with extrajudicial killings. Although the government investigated and prosecuted some cases of extrajudicial killing, an overall lack of accountability for security force abuses remained a problem.

There were numerous reports of politically motivated killings or injuries by the Taliban and other insurgent groups. According to UNAMA's October 19 report, there were 8,397 conflict-related civilian casualties (2,562 deaths and 5,835 injured) between January 1 and September 30, representing a 1 percent decrease from the same period in 2015. The conflict continued to affect the most vulnerable, including women and children. In this same period, UNAMA documented 2,461 child casualties (639 deaths and 1,822 injured), an increase of 15 percent compared with 2015. UNAMA attributed 61 percent of all civilian casualties to nongovernmental elements and 23 percent to progovernment forces.

In July, Human Rights Watch and UNAMA reported that the Afghan army and Junbesh militia forces carried out an operation against the Taliban in Northern Faryab in June in which militia forces killed 13 civilians and wounded 32 others. Human Rights Watch interviewed villagers who said Junbesh fighters entered the villages and targeted those they believed sided with the Taliban.

b. Disappearance

There were reports of disappearances attributed to security forces, and insurgent groups were reportedly also responsible for disappearances and abductions (see section 1.g.).

On November 25, First Vice President General Abdul Rashid Dostum allegedly kidnapped Uzbek tribal elder and political rival Ahmad Ishchi. Before detaining Ishchi, Dostum let his bodyguards brutally beat him during a traditional "buzkashi" match in Jowzan Province. After being held for a number of days, Ishchi later publicized allegations that he was beaten and tortured by Dostum and his men during his detention. The Attorney General's Office opened an investigation into the allegations.

On June 1, Taliban militants kidnapped 17 members of the Hazara Shiite minority community in Sar-e-Pul Province. Although all were subsequently freed, the Taliban continued to target and kidnap members of the Hazara ethnic community, executing Hazara hostages in certain instances. On September 1, Taliban members stopped a car in Dawlat Abad district of Ghor Province and kidnapped five Hazara university students. They killed one of the students and released the other four weeks later.

On August 7, two professors, working for the American University of Afghanistan were kidnapped; at year's end they were still in captivity.

c. Torture and Other Cruel, Inhuman, or Degrading Treatment or Punishment

Although the constitution prohibits such practices, there were reports government officials, security forces, detention center authorities, and police committed abuses. NGOs reported security forces continued to use excessive force, including torturing and beating civilians.

According to local media reports, on July 30, Afghan National Police (ANP) personnel beat civilians in the Speen Ghebarga area of Qalat district in Zabul Province on the site of a recent explosion. The Ministry of Interior suspended three police personnel for the offense.

According to reports, some security officials and persons connected to the ANP raped children with impunity. NGOs reported incidents of sexual abuse and exploitation of children by the Afghan National Defense and Security Forces (ANDSF); however, cultural taboos against reporting such crimes made it difficult to determine the extent of the problem. UNAMA reported it continued to receive allegations of sexual violence against children. In the first half of the year, UNAMA verified two incidents in which ALP used boys for sexual purposes in Baghlan and Kunduz. In one of the cases, an ALP commander in Kunduz kidnapped a 16-year-old boy from his home, brought him to his ALP checkpoint, and raped him for three days. In another case an ALP unit in Baghlan used at least one boy as a bodyguard and for sexual exploitation. There were reports of other boys being abused in the same unit.

There were reports of abuses of power by "arbakai" (untrained local militia) commanders and their followers. According to UNAMA many communities used the terms ALP and arbakai interchangeably, making it difficult to attribute reports of abuses to one group or the other. Nevertheless, credible accounts of killing, rape, assault, the forcible levy of informal taxes, and the traditional practice of "baad" (the transfer of a girl or woman to another family to settle a debt or grievance) were attributed to the ALP.

There were numerous reports of torture and other abuses by the Taliban and other insurgent groups. In March the Afghan Independent Human Rights Commission (AIHRC) reported the Taliban killed a woman in Jowzjan Province for committing adultery, after her husband and his family accused her of having an extramarital affair. Due to security concerns, neither the AIHCRC nor the government was able to investigate the case. In May a video appeared in social media of a woman in Jowzjan Province being tried in an informal Taliban court and later shot in the back of the head and killed.

Prison and Detention Center Conditions

The General Directorate of Prisons and Detention Centers (GDPDC), part of the Ministry of Interior, has responsibility for all civilian-run prisons (for both men and women) and civilian detention centers, including the large national prison complex at Pul-e Charkhi. The Ministry of Justice's Juvenile Rehabilitation Directorate (JRD) is responsible for all juvenile rehabilitation centers. The ANP, which is under the Ministry of Interior, and the National Directorate for Security (NDS), under the ANDSF, also operated short-term detention facilities at the provincial and district levels, usually collocated with their headquarters facilities. The Ministry of Defense runs the Afghan National Detention Facilities at Parwan.

There were reports of private prisons run by members of the ANDSF and used for abuse of detainees.

<u>Physical Conditions</u>: Media and other sources continued to report common inadequacies in food and water and poor sanitation facilities in prisons. Some observers, however, found food and water to be sufficient throughout the GDPDC prisons. The GDPDC's nationwide program to feed prisoners faced a severely limited budget. Many prisoners' families provided food supplements and other necessary items.

Authorities generally lacked the facilities to separate pretrial and convicted inmates, or to separate juveniles according to the seriousness of the charges against them, with the exception of some juvenile facilities that separately housed juveniles imprisoned for national security reasons. According to the UN April 20 *Report on Children in Armed Conflict*, security forces detained hundreds of children on suspicion of being Taliban fighters, attempting suicide attacks, manufacturing or placing IEDs, or assisting insurgent armed groups. In the same report, the United Nations stated the Ministry of Justice reported 214 boys detained in juvenile rehabilitation centers on national security-related charges as of December 2015. There were reports the Parwan detention facility, operated by the Ministry of Defense, held 145 children for security-related offenses ay year's end, a threefold increase compared with the previous year.

Overcrowding in prisons continued to be a serious, widespread problem; 28 of 34 provincial prisons for men were severely overcrowded, based on standards recommended by the International Committee of the Red Cross. As of July men's prison facilities were at approximately 190 percent of capacity across the country. The Kapisa provincial prison for men was the most overcrowded, housing 340 inmates, more than 10 times the 29 prisoners for which it was designed. The country's largest prison, Pul-e Charkhi, held 12,398 prisoners as of September, which was more than double the number it was designed to house.

In a March assessment on the country's prison health services, UNAMA reported that few prisoners had access to medical check-ups or psychiatric services. The report also suggested the 26 provincial prisons did not have the female medical staff necessary to treat female prisoners. As a result, many children, up to the age of seven, accompanied their mothers to prison. In the same assessment, UNAMA reported that 336 children were accompanying female prisoners held in provincial prisons. While many women opted to keep their children with them in prison (ages seven and under), many others enrolled their children in Child Support Centers (CSCs). There were three CSCs: in Kabul, Mazar, and Herat.

In March, after authorities moved the Kabul Female Prison and Detention Center from a renovated building in the city to an allegedly subpar facility in the Pul-e Charkhi prison complex, a group of female prisoners set the facility on fire to protest their new living conditions.

Administration: The law provides prisoners with the right to leave prison for up to 20 days for family visits. Most prisons did not implement this provision, and the law is unclear in its application to different classes of prisoners.

Independent Monitoring: The AIHRC, UNAMA, and International Committee of the Red Cross continued to have access to detention facilities of the NDS and the Ministries of Interior, Justice, and Defense, and NATO Mission Resolute Support had access to NDS, ANP, and Ministry of Defense facilities. Security constraints and obstruction by authorities occasionally prevented visits to some places of detention. UNAMA and the AIHRC reported difficulty accessing NDS places of detention when unannounced. While Resolute Support did not experience the same level of difficulty, authorities denied unannounced access on several occasions at NDS and ANP facilities. The AIHRC reported NDS officials usually required the AIHRC to submit a formal letter requesting access at least one to two days in advance of a visit. NDS officials continued to prohibit AIHRC and UNAMA monitors from bringing cameras, mobile phones, recording devices, or computers into NDS facilities, thereby preventing AIHRC monitors from properly documenting physical evidence of abuse, such as bruises, scars, and other injuries. The NDS assigned a colonel to monitor human rights conditions in its facilities. In February and May, members of parliament visited GDPDC prison facilities to conduct monitoring and oversight of prison conditions, with a focus on conditions for women. The Justice Ministry's JRD also produced an annual report in March on juvenile justice problems, drafted by the JRD's Monitoring and Evaluation Office.

d. Arbitrary Arrest or Detention

The law prohibits arbitrary arrest or detention, but both remained serious problems. Authorities detained many citizens without respecting essential procedural protections.

According to NGOs, law enforcement officers continued to detain citizens arbitrarily without clear legal authority or due process. Local law enforcement officials reportedly detained persons illegally on charges not provided for in the penal code. In 2012 the Attorney General's Office (AGO) ordered a halt to the prosecution of women for "running away," which is not a crime under the law. Reports indicated that prosecutors instead charged women who had left home with "attempted zina" (extramarital sexual relations) for being outside the home in the presence of nonrelated men, which is also not a crime under the law. In some cases authorities wrongfully imprisoned women because they deemed it unsafe for the women to return home or because women's shelters were not available to provide protection in the provinces or districts at issue (see section 6, Women).

Role of the Police and Security Apparatus

Three ministries have responsibility for providing security in the country, the Ministry of Interior, the Ministry of Defense, and the NDS. The ANP, under the Interior Ministry, has primary responsibility for internal order and also has responsibility for the ALP, a community-based self-defense force. The Afghan National Army (ANA), under the Ministry of Defense, is responsible for external security, but its primary activity is fighting the insurgency internally. The NDS functions as an intelligence agency and has responsibility for investigating criminal cases concerning national security. The investigative branch of the NDS operated a facility in Kabul, where it held national security prisoners awaiting trial until their cases were transferred to prosecutors. In some areas insurgents, rather than the ANP or ANA, maintained control.

There were reports of impunity and lack of accountability by security forces throughout the year. According to observers, ALP and ANP personnel were largely unaware of their responsibilities and defendants' rights under the law. Accountability of NDS and ANP officials for torture and abuse was weak, not transparent, and rarely enforced. Independent judicial or external oversight of the NDS and ANP in the investigation and prosecution of crimes or misconduct, including torture and abuse, was limited. Police corruption remained a serious problem (see section 4).

NGOs and human rights activists reported widespread societal violence, especially against women (see section 6). In many cases police did not prevent or respond to violence and, in some cases, arrested women who reported crimes committed against them, such as rape.

Arrest Procedures and Treatment of Detainees

UNAMA, the AIHRC, and other observers reported arbitrary and prolonged detention frequently occurred throughout the country. Authorities often did not inform detainees of the charges against them.

The law provides for access to legal counsel and the use of warrants, and it limits how long authorities may hold detainees without charge. Police have the right to detain a suspect for 72 hours to complete a preliminary investigation. If police decide to pursue a case, they transfer the file to the AGO. With court approval the investigating prosecutor may continue to detain a suspect while continuing the investigation, with the length of continued detention depending on the severity of the offense. The investigating prosecutor may detain a suspect for a maximum of 10 additional days for a petty crime, 27 days for a misdemeanor, and 75 days for a felony. The prosecutor must file an indictment or release the suspect within those deadlines, and no further extension of the investigatory period is permitted if the defendant is in detention. Prosecutors often ignored these limits.

Incommunicado imprisonment remained a problem, and prompt access to a lawyer was rare. Prisoners generally were allowed access to their families, but there were exceptions, and access was frequently delayed.

The criminal procedure code does provide for release on bail; however, in practice, the bond system was not always used. Authorities at times continued to detain defendants who had been acquitted by the courts on the grounds that defendants who were released pending the prosecution's appeal often disappeared. In many cases authorities did not rearrest defendants they released pending the outcome of an appeal, even after the appellate court convicted them in absentia.

According to international monitors, prosecutors filed indictments in cases transferred to them by police, even where there was a reasonable belief no crime was actually committed.

According to the juvenile code, the arrest of a child "should be a matter of last resort and should last for the shortest possible period." Reports indicated children in juvenile rehabilitation centers across the country lacked access to adequate food, health care, and education. Like adult detainees, detained children frequently were denied basic rights and many aspects of due process, including the presumption of innocence, the right to be informed of charges, access to defense lawyers, and protection from self-incrimination. The law provides for the creation of special juvenile police, prosecution offices, and courts. Due to limited resources, special juvenile courts functioned in only six provinces (Kabul, Herat, Balkh, Kandahar,

Nangarhar, and Kunduz). Elsewhere, children's cases fall under the ordinary courts. The law mandates that authorities handle children's cases confidentially and, as with all criminal cases, may involve three stages: primary, appeals, and the final stage at the Supreme Court.

Some children in the criminal justice system were victims rather than perpetrators of crime. In some instances authorities chose to punish victims because they brought shame on the family by reporting an abuse. In the absence of sufficient shelters for boys, authorities detained abused boys and placed them in juvenile rehabilitation centers because they could not be returned to their families and shelter elsewhere was unavailable. There were also allegations that authorities allegedly treated children related to a perpetrator as proxies and imprisoned them.

Police and legal officials often charged women with intent to commit zina to justify their arrest and incarceration for social offenses, such as running away from home, rejecting a spouse chosen by her family, fleeing domestic violence or rape, or eloping. Article 130 of the constitution provides that in cases not explicitly covered by the provisions of the constitution or other laws, courts may, in accordance with Hanafi jurisprudence (a school of sharia, or Islamic law) and within the limits set by the constitution, rule in a manner that best attains justice in the case. Although observers stated this provision was widely understood to apply only to civil cases, many judges and prosecutors applied Article 130 to criminal matters. Observers reported officials used this article to charge women and men with "immorality" or "running away from home," neither of which is a crime. Police often detained women for zina at the request of family members.

Authorities imprisoned some women for reporting crimes perpetrated against them and detained some as proxies for a husband or male relative convicted of a crime on the assumption the suspect would turn himself in to free the family member.

Authorities placed some women in protective custody to prevent violence by family members. They also employed protective custody (including placement in a detention center) for women who had experienced domestic violence, if no shelters were available to protect them from further abuse. The presidential decree on the Elimination of Violence Against Women (EVAW)--commonly referred to as the EVAW law--obliges police to arrest persons who abuse women. Implementation and awareness of the EVAW law was limited, however.

<u>Arbitrary Arrest</u>: Arbitrary arrest and detention remained a problem in most provinces. Observers reported some prosecutors and police detained individuals

without charge for actions that were not crimes under the law, in part because the judicial system was inadequate to process detainees in a timely fashion. UNAMA reported police detained individuals for moral crimes, breach of contract, family disputes, and to extract confessions. Observers continued to report those detained for moral crimes were almost exclusively women.

<u>Pretrial Detention</u>: The law provides a defendant the right to object to his or her pretrial detention and receive a court hearing on the matter. Nevertheless, lengthy pretrial detention remained a problem.

Many detainees did not benefit from any or all of the provisions of the criminal procedure code, largely due to a lack of resources, limited numbers of defense attorneys, unskilled legal practitioners, and corruption. The law provides that, if the investigation cannot be completed or an indictment is not filed, within the code's 10-, 27-, or 75-day deadlines, the defendant must be released. Many detainees, however, were held beyond those periods, despite the lack of an indictment.

<u>Amnesty</u>: The Afghanistan Peace and Reintegration Program, which existed between 2010 and 2016, was a mechanism for bringing combatants off the battlefield. The program document stated the program "is not a framework for pardoning all crimes and providing blanket amnesty," and reintegration candidates were informed prior to enrollment that entry into the program did not amount to blanket immunity from prosecution.

In September the government concluded a peace accord with the Hezb-e Islami Gulbuddin group. As part of the agreement, the government pledged to release certain prisoners in its custody. At year's end the government was vetting prisoners for possible release.

As of September 2015, prison industries offered more jobs and vocational training to enhance employment opportunities after release. In December 2015 President Ghani visited Badam Bagh prison in Kabul to inquire about the situation of female inmates. Ghani said he personally oversaw the drafting of pardon and parole decrees and ordered the creation of an impartial delegation composed of female representatives from civil society to look into female prisoners' cases. The delegation, comprising nine women, was reviewing female inmate cases to ensure those eligible were released. By year's end, 235 women had been released, and 307 had their sentences reduced.

e. Denial of Fair Public Trial

The law provides for an independent judiciary, but the judiciary continued to be underfunded, understaffed, inadequately trained, largely ineffective, and subject to threats, bias, political influence, and pervasive corruption.

Bribery, corruption, and pressure from public officials, tribal leaders, families of accused persons, and individuals associated with the insurgency continued to impair judicial impartiality. Most courts administered justice unevenly, employing a mixture of codified law, sharia, and local custom. Traditional justice mechanisms remained the main recourse for many, especially in rural areas. There was varying adherence to codified law, with courts often disregarding applicable statutory law in favor of sharia or local custom. Corruption was common within the judiciary, and often criminals paid bribes to obtain their release or a reduction in sentence (see section 4).

The formal justice system was relatively strong in urban centers, where the central government was strongest, and weaker in rural areas, where approximately 76 percent of the population lived. Courts and police forces continued to operate at less than full strength nationwide. The judicial system continued to lack the capacity to absorb and implement the large volume of new and amended legislation. A lack of qualified judicial personnel hindered the courts. Some municipal and provincial authorities, including judges, had minimal training and often based their judgments on their personal understanding of sharia without appropriate reference to statutory law, tribal codes of honor, or local custom. The number of judges who were graduates of law school, many from universities with sharia faculties, continued to increase. Access to legal codes and statutes increased, but their limited availability continued to hinder some judges and prosecutors.

In March 2015 a mob killed Farkhunda Malikzada after a local religious cleric falsely accused her of burning a copy of the Quran. Following protests after Farkhunda's death, the government promised swift and exemplary justice but showed little progress in holding the attackers accountable. A court prosecuted some of the attackers and sentenced some to the death penalty. In March 2016, however, the Supreme Court voted to reduce the sentences of those convicted. The reasoning was that the death penalty can be imposed only where the accused are found to be the "main perpetrators" of the death. The Supreme Court held it could not find sufficient evidence that any of the four men were the direct cause of Farkhunda's death.

Following the Supreme Court decision to uphold the reduced sentences, President Ghani established an investigatory committee to look into Farkhunda's case. More than 40 civil society and women's organizations formed an alliance to demand that the Supreme Court decision be investigated and revisited. As an example, the Women's Political Participation Committee, a civil society organization, held a press conference on March 19 to call on the government to reassess the Supreme Court's decision and ensure more transparency in the process.

There was a widespread shortage of judges, primarily in insecure areas. UNAMA reported Taliban attacks against judicial authorities and prosecutors significantly increased following the government's execution on May 8 of six Taliban prisoners. Following the executions, the Taliban carried out major attacks against judicial officials. On May 25, a Taliban suicide bomber attacked a government shuttle bus transporting Maidan Wardak provincial court staff members, killing 12 civilians, including two judges, and injuring nine others. On June 1, the Taliban attacked Ghazni's provincial appellate court and killed four civilians, including two court staff, and injured 15 others, including the head of the court.

In major cities, courts continued to decide criminal cases as mandated by law. Civil cases continued to be frequently resolved using the informal system or, in some cases, through negotiations between the parties facilitated by judicial personnel or private lawyers. Because the formal legal system often was not present in rural areas, local elders and shuras (consultative gatherings, usually of men selected by the community) were the primary means of settling both criminal matters and civil disputes. They also imposed punishments without regard to the formal legal system.

In some areas the Taliban enforced a parallel judicial system based on a strict interpretation of sharia. Punishments could include execution or mutilation. For example, in August in Kapisa Province, the Taliban accused a 20-year-old student of spying, kidnapped him, and killed him a week later. UNAMA reported death sentences, lashings, and beatings resulted in 29 civilian casualties (24 deaths and five injuries) in the first half of the year, a 28 percent increase over the same period in the previous year.

Trial Procedures

The constitution provides the right to a fair and public trial, but the judiciary rarely enforced this provision. The administration and implementation of justice varied in different areas of the country. The government formally uses an inquisitorial legal system. By law all citizens are entitled to a presumption of innocence, and those accused have the right to be present at trial and to appeal, although these rights were not always respected. In some provinces public trials were held, but this was not the norm. Three-judge panels decide criminal trials, and there is no right to a jury trial under the constitution. Prosecutors rarely informed defendants promptly and in detail of the charges brought against them. An indigent defendant has the right to consult with an advocate or counsel at public expense when resources allow. This right was applied inconsistently, in large part due to a severe shortage of defense lawyers. Citizens often were unaware of their constitutional rights. Defendants and attorneys were entitled to examine physical evidence and documents related to a case before trial, although observers noted court documents often were not available for review before cases went to trial, despite defense lawyers' requests.

Criminal defense attorneys reported justice system officials were slowly demonstrating increased respect and tolerance for the role of defense lawyers in criminal trials, but at times defendants' attorneys experienced abuse and threats from prosecutors and other law enforcement officials.

The criminal procedure code establishes time limits for the completion of each stage of a criminal case, from investigation through final appeal, when an accused is in custody. The code also allows for the accused persons to be released temporarily on bail, but this was rarely used. An addendum to the code provides for extended custodial limits in cases involving crimes committed against the internal and external security of the country. Courts at the Justice Center in Parwan elected to utilize the extended time periods. If the deadlines are not met, the law requires the accused be released from custody. In many cases courts did not meet these deadlines, but detainees nevertheless remained in custody.

In cases where no clearly defined legal statute applied, or where judges, prosecutors, or elders were unaware of the statutory law, judges and informal shuras enforced customary law. This practice often resulted in outcomes that discriminated against women.

Political Prisoners and Detainees

There were no reports the government held political prisoners or detainees.

Civil Judicial Procedures and Remedies

Citizens had limited access to justice for constitutional and human rights violations. The state judiciary did not play a significant or effective role in adjudicating civil matters due to corruption and lack of capacity, although the judiciary frequently adjudicated family law matters.

f. Arbitrary Interference with Privacy, Family, Home, or Correspondence

The law prohibits arbitrary interference in matters of privacy, but authorities did not always respect its provisions. The criminal procedure code contains additional safeguards for the privacy of the home, prohibiting night arrests and strengthening requirements for body searches. The government did not always respect these prohibitions.

Government officials continued to enter homes and businesses of civilians forcibly and without legal authorization.

There were reports that government officials monitored private communications, including telephone calls and other digital communications, without legal authority or judicial warrant.

Authorities imprisoned relatives, male and female, of criminal suspects and escaped convicts in order to induce the persons being sought to surrender (see section 1.d.).

Insurgents continued to intimidate cell phone operators to shut down operations. Reports of destruction of mobile telephone towers, bribing of guards, and disconnecting of networks at night were particularly common in the southwestern, southern, and eastern provinces.

g. Abuses in Internal Conflict

Continuing internal conflict resulted in civilian deaths, abductions, prisoner abuse, property damage, displacement of residents, and other abuses. The security situation remained a problem due to insurgent attacks. Civilians, particularly women and children, continued to bear the brunt of intensified armed conflict, according to UNAMA. Overall civilian casualties continued at approximately the same rates as in 2015, but with a 1 percent decrease in deaths. Terrorist groups caused the vast majority of civilian deaths.

<u>Killings</u>: For the first nine months of the year, UNAMA documented 8,397 civilian casualties (2,562 deaths and 5,835 injured). UNAMA attributed 23 percent of civilian casualties to progovernment forces, while it attributed 61 percent of all civilian casualties to antigovernment elements.

According to UNAMA, ground engagements and crossfire incidents involving the parties to the conflict remained the largest cause of civilian casualties (dead and injured), followed by suicide and complex attacks and IEDs. UNAMA reported that the number of casualties among children in the first nine months of the year increased by 15 percent over the same period in 2015. Antigovernment elements continued to use suicide and complex attacks to target civilians and government officials, a practice that became the most harmful tactic by antigovernment forces. In the first nine months of the year, suicide and complex attacks represented 20 percent of all civilian casualties, while IEDs caused 18 percent of casualties.

The increase in complex and suicide attacks was evidenced by the attack in Kabul in July, when a twin bombing occurred near Deh Mazang Square in Kabul during a peaceful demonstration. More than 80 demonstrators, predominantly Shiite Hazara, were killed by the blasts, and more than 230 were injured.

Antigovernment elements continued to attack religious leaders whom they concluded spoke against the insurgency or the Taliban. Antigovernment elements also continued to target government officials. The majority of Taliban attacks targeted security forces, in particular ANP and ALP forces, notably in volatile areas. Antigovernment elements continued to use civilian residences to attack government forces, such as those that occurred in February in Dand E Ghori, according to local media.

The Taliban and antigovernment elements continued to engage in indiscriminate use of force, attacking and killing villagers, foreigners, and NGO workers in armed attacks and with vehicle-borne improvised explosive devices (VBIEDs) and suicide bombs. Through the first six months of the year, UNAMA documented 2,509 civilian casualties (531 civilian deaths and 1,528 injuries) because of combined IED tactics, or 67 percent of all civilian casualties caused by antigovernment forces.

<u>Abductions</u>: UNAMA documented 195 incidents of conflict-related abductions in the first six months of the year that resulted in 85 civilian casualties (46 deaths and 39 injured) and the abduction of 1,141 persons. This showed a 67 percent increase in the number of civilians abducted, albeit with a 2 percent decrease in the overall

number of abductions, compared with the same period in 2015. On May 30, the Taliban stopped three civilian buses carrying passengers from Kabul to Takhar and Badakhshan Provinces in Ali Abad district of Kunduz Province. Taliban abducted 185 passengers, including 30 women and children. The abductors identified 28 men as Afghan Security Personnel and released 157 passengers. They executed 12 of the kidnapped passengers and released eight others. The last eight were released a month and a half later, after local elders mediated their release.

Physical Abuse, Punishment, and Torture: According to some reports, on June 26, security forces launched a combined operation with progovernment armed groups against the Taliban in Faryab Province. While the Taliban fled the area, progovernment armed groups led by six commanders conducted operations in four villages that resulted in 17 casualties (five deaths and 12 injured). The forces loyal to these six commanders shot and killed three civilian men in Sheshpar village and severely beat 14 other men in the same village on accusation of supporting the Taliban; two of the 14 beaten men died of their wounds. There were reports that these forces looted and burned civilian houses in Shordarya area, and UNAMA was investigating the allegations. President Ghani ordered the arrest of individuals responsible for the abuse, and the NDS arrested one commander and seven men while the investigation continued.

Antigovernment elements continued to target civilians. The following are illustrative examples. In February, Taliban members killed four civilians at a wedding party in the Sar Hakwza district of Paktika Province, accusing them of cooperating with government officials. On March 5, the Taliban shot and killed a mosque custodian/imam in front of his mosque in Kandahar Province. The group claimed that the imam was working for the government's intelligence service.

Land mines, unexploded ordnance, and explosive remnants of war (ERW) continued to cause deaths and injuries, restrict areas available for farming, and impede the return of refugees. UNAMA reported the number of deaths and injuries from land mines, unexploded ordnance, and explosive remnants of war was 35 percent higher than in previous years. The Mine Action Program of Afghanistan reported that during the 12 months ending in March, there were 155 reported casualties from ERW, seven casualties due to land mines, and 1,051 casualties from pressure-plate improvised explosive devices (PPIEDs). In addition to these casualties from traditional antitank and antipersonnel mines and PPIEDs, there continued to be thousands of civilian casualties from other IEDs. According to the Mine Action Coordination Center, land mines, unexploded ordnance, and ERW imperiled 1,577 communities across 256 districts, covering approximately

230 square miles. The Ministry of Education and NGOs continued to conduct educational programs and mine awareness campaigns throughout the country.

Between January 1 and June 30, child casualties from ERW increased by 53 percent, accounting for 85 percent of all civilian casualties caused by ERW, compared with the same period in 2015. ERW caused 264 child casualties (83 deaths and 181 injured), making it the second leading cause of child casualties in the first half of the year. In the same period, UNAMA documented 136 incidents of ERW detonation resulting in 312 civilian casualties (95 deaths and 217 injured, a 49 percent increase compared with the first half of 2015. Mine-risk education, in collaboration with the Ministry of Education, was conducted in schools to raise awareness. According to the Mine Action Program Coordination Center of Afghanistan, there were 1,620 mine-contaminated communities, covering an area of approximately 210 square miles.

Child Soldiers: There were reports the ANDSF and progovernment militias, particularly the ANP and ALP, recruited and used children for military purposes. In an effort to prevent the recruitment of children, the government continued to work towards the expansion of Child Protection Units (CPUs) to all 34 provinces. As of November there were 17 active CPUs--12 of them established during the year. According to the UN Children's Fund (UNICEF), CPUs prevented 315 children from being recruited during the year.

The AIHRC reported 21 cases of child recruitment by the Ministry of Interior security forces. Under a government action plan, the ANP took steps that included training staff on age-assessment procedures, launching an awareness campaign on underage recruitment, investigating alleged cases of underage recruitment, and establishing centers in some provincial recruitment centers to document cases of attempted enlistment by children. Recruits undergo an identity check, including a requirement that at least two community elders vouch that a recruit is 18 years old and is eligible to join the ANDSF. The Ministries of Interior and Defense also issued directives meant to prevent the recruitment and sexual abuse of children by the ANDSF. Media reported in some cases ANDSF units used children as personal servants, support staff, or for sexual purposes.

UNAMA also documented the recruitment of children by the Taliban and other antigovernment elements, although figures were unreliable and difficult to obtain. In some cases the Taliban and other antigovernment elements used children as suicide bombers and human shields and in other cases to assist with their work, such as placing IEDs, particularly in southern provinces. Media, NGOs, and UN agencies reported the Taliban tricked children, promised them money, used false religious pretexts, or forced them to become suicide bombers. During the year the United Nations recorded 35 cases of child recruitment by armed opposition groups and 13 cases by the ANDSF.

In February the Taliban killed Wasil Ahmad, an 11-year-old boy who had been praised for fighting in an ALP unit for 43 days in 2015 when Taliban forces laid siege to his hometown of Khas Uruzgan. Although the ALP claimed the boy was not recruited and volunteered to defend his family, he was armed and in uniform. The boy was killed six months after the siege; he was no longer engaged in combat.

Also see the Department of State's annual *Trafficking in Persons Report* at www.state.gov/j/tip/rls/tiprpt/.

Other Conflict-related Abuse: The security environment continued to have a negative effect on the ability of humanitarian organizations to operate freely in many parts of the country. Insurgents deliberately targeted government employees and aid workers.

Suspected Taliban members attacked NGO offices, vehicles, guesthouses, restaurants, and hotels frequented by NGO employees. Violence and instability hampered development, relief, and reconstruction efforts. NGOs reported insurgents, powerful local individuals, and militia leaders demanded bribes to allow groups to bring relief supplies into the country and distribute them. In April unidentified armed men abducted 15 members of a mine removal team from HALO Trust, a mine-clearing agency, in Herat Province. The men were released the next day during a military operation.

The Taliban continued to distribute threatening messages in attempts to curtail government and development activities. Insurgents used civilians, including children, as human shields, either by forcing them into the line of fire or by conducting operations in civilian settings.

In the south and east, the Taliban and other antigovernment elements frequently forced local residents to provide food and shelter for their fighters. The Taliban also continued to attack schools, radio stations, and government offices.

On September 5, Taliban forces carried out two large bombing operations in Kabul, targeting the Ministry of Defense and the humanitarian agency CARE

International. At least 30 were killed and more than 90 injured at the ministry.
The majority of casualties at the ministry attack were ANDSF, and an ANA
general and two senior police officials were among the dead. The Taliban
immediately claimed responsibility for the attack. At CARE International
unidentified attackers detonated a VBIED at the agency's headquarters. One
civilian was killed, while one ANP person and seven civilians were injured.

On October 25, militants killed 24 civilians--including women and children--who
had been captured the day before near the Ghor provincial capital of Firezkoh city
(formerly Chaghcharan). The Taliban denied involvement, and the provincial
governor's spokesperson told one journalist that Islamic State in Khorasan
Province carried out the attack. Other reports indicated the civilians were executed
in response to the death of local Taliban commander Faroq on October 24 during
an attack on an Afghan National Civil Order Police checkpoint.

Section 2. Respect for Civil Liberties, Including:

a. Freedom of Speech and Press

The constitution provides for freedom of speech and of the press, but the
government sometimes restricted these rights to varying degrees.

Freedom of Speech and Expression: While the law provides for freedom of
speech, which was widely exercised, there were reports authorities at times used
pressure, regulations, and threats to silence critics. Freedom of speech was also
considerably more constrained at the provincial level, where local power brokers,
such as former mujahedin-era military leaders, exerted significant influence and
authority to intimidate or threaten their critics, both private citizens and journalists.

Press and Media Freedoms: While media reported independently throughout the
year, often openly criticizing the government, full press freedoms were lacking. At
times authorities used pressure, regulations, and threats to silence critics.
Politicians, security officials, and others in positions of power arrested, threatened,
or harassed journalists because of their coverage. Freedom of speech and an
independent media were even more constrained at the provincial level, where
many media outlets had links to specific personalities or political parties, to include
former mujahedin military leaders who owned many of the broadcasting stations
and print media and influenced their content.

Print media continued to publish independent magazines, newsletters, and newspapers. A wide range of editorials and dailies openly criticized the government. There were concerns, however, that media independence and safety remained at high risk in light of increased attacks. Due to high levels of illiteracy, television and radio were the preferred information source for most citizens. Radio remained more widespread due to its relative accessibility, with approximately 75 percent radio penetration, compared with approximately 50 percent for television.

The Ministry of Information and Culture has authority to regulate the press and media. In 2015 the ministry dissolved the Media Violations Investigation Commission, whose evaluations of complaints against journalists were criticized as biased and not based on the law. Human Rights Watch reported the ministry routinely ignored officials who threatened, intimidated, or even physically attacked members of the press. While the ministry has legal responsibility for regulating media, the council of religious scholars (the Ulema Council) had considerable influence over media affairs.

In January the information ministry created the Independent Mass Media Commission. The commission is responsible for reregistering all media outlets in the country. Media activists condemned the new reregistration process, citing the high fees to undergo the process would hurt media outlets, particularly the smaller radio and television stations in the provinces. As of September media advocates had been able to delay the implementation of the new reregistration regulation.

In February, after the president issued a decree to implement current media laws and strengthen freedom of expression, the executive created a committee to investigate cases of violence against journalists. The committee met multiple times in the first half of the year and identified 432 cases eligible for investigation. The committee sent the cases to the appropriate government institutions associated with the violations for investigation, including the Ministry of Interior and NDS forces. As of September none of the government institutions had started an investigation or provided a response to the committee.

In May parliament members criticized the lack of full implementation of the 2014 Access to Information law. The Commission on Monitoring Access to Information stated a lack of budget and lack of government support resulted in weak implementation of the law.

Violence and Harassment: Government used threats, violence, and intimidation to silence opposition journalists, particularly those who spoke out about impunity, war crimes, government officials, and powerful local figures. The AJSC reported that 50 percent of 101 incidents of attacks against journalists, including 13 cases of killings, 30 cases of beatings, 35 cases of intimidation, 17 cases of abuse, and six cases of injury, were attributed to government officials. In an October 30 press conference, Nai, an NGO supporting media freedom, reported that violence against media workers had increased to approximately 370 cases, in comparison with 95 cases in 2015. According to Nai, nearly 300 journalists left their jobs during the year due to threats. For example, according to reports, on June 5, police beat a reporter from Kawoon Ghag Radio while he reporting on an event where donations were distributed to poor families.

On August 29, while the president visited Bamyan Province to inaugurate the refurbished provincial airport, progovernment forces, including the president's protective detail, allegedly harassed and beat protesters and journalists. Some journalists reported government security forces used violence against them and removed film or digital photographs from their equipment. Human Rights Watch received reports of NDS forces detaining journalists and activists for 24 hours. The Presidential Palace first rejected claims of journalists being beaten or detained during the August Bamyan visit, but later the president ordered an investigation.

On August 28, the leading independent daily newspaper, *Hasht-e-Subh*, intentionally left an entire page empty of content in all Herat city editions to highlight censorship of a news feature detailing corruption and smuggling allegations against Herat provincial council chief Kamran Alizai. The newspaper's editor in chief, Parwiz Kawa, publicly stated the blank page demonstrated what he termed was a "preventive and protective" protest against an unnamed "powerful official." He said editors were responding to threats against their regional offices by Alizai, who also maintained an illegal private militia. On the following day, *Hasht-e-Subh* published an article claiming the AGO assured editors that Alizai was under investigation, had been suspended from his duties, and had been banned from leaving the country. In the meantime the president's deputy spokesperson, Shah Hussain Murtazawi, told *Hasht-e-Subh,* "Anyone who challenges independent media would be harshly confronted by the government."

Prevailing security conditions created a dangerous environment for journalists, even when they were not specific targets. Media organizations and journalists operating in remote areas were more vulnerable to violence and intimidation because of the increased level of insecurity and pronounced fear from insurgents, warlords, and organized criminals. They also reported local governmental authorities were less cooperative in facilitating access to information.

On August 24, the National Security Council approved a new set of guidelines to address cases of violence against journalists. The new initiative entails the creation of a joint national committee in Kabul and separate committees in provincial capitals, a coordination center to investigate and identify perpetrators of violence against journalists, and a support committee to be run by the NDS to identify threats against journalists. The joint committee, to be chaired by the second vice president, was expected to register new cases, call for support from judicial bodies to prosecute perpetrators, and publicly share statistics on cases. Activists welcomed the government's initiative.

An independent organization focused on the safety of journalists continued to operate a safe house for journalists facing threats. It reported law enforcement officials generally cooperated in assisting journalists who faced credible threats, although limited investigative capacity meant many cases remained unresolved. The Afghan Independent Bar Association established a media law committee to provide legal support, expertise, and services to media organizations.

Women constituted approximately 20 percent of media workers, compared with 30 percent in 2015. Some women oversaw radio stations across the country, and some radio stations emphasized almost exclusively female concerns. Nevertheless, female reporters found it difficult to practice their profession. Poor security, lack of training, and unsafe working conditions limited the participation of women in the media. The AJSC released a special report in March on the situation of female journalists, noting that sexual harassment continued to be wide spread in the media industry. If not subjected to sexual harassment and abuse at work, female journalists often faced pressure by their families to leave the media profession or at least not to show their faces on television.

Censorship or Content Restrictions: The government reportedly sought to restrict reporting on topics deemed contrary to the government's messaging.

Some media observers claimed journalists reporting on administrative corruption, land embezzlement, and local officials' involvement in narcotics trafficking engaged in self-censorship due to fear of violent retribution by provincial police officials and powerful families. Fearing retribution by government officials, media outlets sometimes preferred to quote from foreign media reports on sensitive topics and in some cases fed stories to foreign journalists.

Nai conducted a survey in Kabul and five different provinces that revealed 94 percent of local social media users practiced self-censorship, fearing security threats and intimidation,

Libel Laws: The penal code and the mass media law prescribe jail sentences and fines for defamation. Authorities sometime used defamation as a pretext to suppress criticism of government officials.

National Security: Journalists complained government officials frequently invoked the national interest exception in the Access to Information law to avoid disclosing certain information.

Nongovernmental Impact: Journalists continued to face threats from the Taliban and other insurgents. Some reporters acknowledged they avoided criticizing the insurgency and some neighboring countries in their reporting because they feared Taliban retribution. In February, two Afghan Adib radio workers in Pol-e Khomri in Baghlan Province were brutally attacked, leaving one in a coma. Taliban forces reportedly were behind the attack, although no group claimed responsibility.

The Committee to Protect Journalists reported local and foreign reporters continued to be at risk of kidnapping.

The Taliban continued to threaten journalists associated with two privately owned Afghan television outlets, ToloNews TV, and 1TV. The Taliban's military commission designated both outlets as "military objectives" due to their perceived disrespectful coverage and claims that they broadcast propaganda, ridiculed religion, and injected the minds of youth with immorality. The Taliban for the first time openly threatened ToloNews in 2015, after the news channel reported allegations of executions, rape, kidnappings, and other abuses by the Taliban when Kunduz fell to the antigovernment group. On January 20, a Taliban suicide bomber in Kabul targeted and struck a minibus carrying Kaboora production staff, an affiliate of ToloNews, killing seven. On June 8, unknown gunmen launched a grenade attack on Enikas Radio in Jalalabad, just three days after an American journalist and a translator embedded in a local security forces convoy were killed by an ambush in Helmand Province on June 5.

Internet Freedom

The government did not restrict or disrupt access to the internet, and there were no credible reports that the government monitored private online communications without appropriate legal authority.

Media outlets and activists routinely used social media to discuss political developments, and Facebook was widely used in urban areas. The Taliban used the internet and social media (for example, Twitter) to spread its messages. Internet usage remained relatively low due to high prices, inadequate local content, and illiteracy.

Academic Freedom and Cultural Events

There were no reports that the government imposed restrictions on academic freedom or cultural events during the year.

b. Freedom of Peaceful Assembly and Association

Freedom of Assembly

The government generally respected citizens' right to demonstrate peacefully. Numerous public gatherings and protests took place during the year. In May a mass demonstration took place in Kabul over the government's decision on routing of an electricity line from Turkmenistan to Kabul. Although government forces placed shipping containers to provide security and limited the areas in which the demonstration took place, protesters were allowed to march on the streets of Kabul. On July 23, protesters gathered again to protest the same electricity line but were attacked by insurgents with a bomb that killed 80 and injured an additional 250 protesters. After Da'esh claimed responsibility, the Ministry of Interior banned street protests for 10 days.

In September, Tajik supporters assembled to rebury the remains of a former king on a hill important to the Uzbek community in Kabul, leading to a standoff. After an agreement was reached, the reburial took place, although some criticized the government for not handling the issue properly.

Freedom of Association

The right to freedom of association is provided in the constitution, and the government generally respected it. The 2009 law on political parties obliges them to register with the Ministry of Justice and to pursue objectives consistent with

Islam. By law a political party must have 10,000 registered members to register with the ministry.

In 2012 the Council of Ministers approved a regulation requiring political parties to open offices in at least 20 provinces within one year of registration. The regulation provides for removal of parties failing to do so from the Justice Ministry's official list. In 2015 the ministry conducted a nationwide review of provincial political party offices. It found 10 political parties not in compliance with the regulation and deregistered all 10 of them. There were a total of 57 political parties registered with the ministry.

c. Freedom of Religion

See the Department of State's *International Religious Freedom Report* at www.state.gov/religiousfreedomreport/.

d. Freedom of Movement, Internally Displaced Persons, Protection of Refugees, and Stateless Persons

The law provides for freedom of internal movement, foreign travel, emigration, and repatriation, which the government generally respected, although it sometimes limited citizens' movement for security reasons.

The government cooperated with the Office of the UN High Commissioner for Refugees (UNHCR), the International Organization for Migration, and other humanitarian organizations in providing protection and assistance to internally displaced persons (IDPs), refugees, returning refugees, and other persons of concern. Government ability to assist vulnerable persons, including returnees from Pakistan and Iran, remained limited, and it continued to rely on the international community for assistance.

In-country Movement: Taxi, truck, and bus drivers reported security forces or insurgents sometimes operated illegal checkpoints and extorted money and goods from travelers.

The greatest barrier to movement in some parts of the country was the lack of security. In many areas insurgent violence, banditry, land mines, and IEDs made travel extremely dangerous, especially at night.

Armed insurgents operated illegal checkpoints and extorted money and goods. The Taliban imposed nightly curfews on the local populace in regions where it exercised authority, mostly in the southeast.

Social custom limited women's freedom of movement without male consent or a male chaperone.

Emigration and Repatriation: Refugee returns to the country rose in the last half of the year. As of mid-November UNHCR had assisted the return of more than 370,000 registered refugees (99 percent of whom returned from Pakistan), greatly surpassing the 58,460 returns in 2015. According to UNHCR surveys of returnees at arrival centers, many returnees claimed they left Pakistan due to increased rates of harassment and extortion and because they no longer believed they could stay in their homes safely or find jobs. Other reasons they cited included maintaining family unity with undocumented Afghans following their deportation, enhanced border controls, and uncertainty about legal status. Former refugees constituted more than 20 percent of the total country population, yet the government lacked the capacity to integrate large numbers of new arrivals due to continuing insecurity, limited employment opportunities, poor development, and budgetary constraints.

Undocumented Afghan refugees also returned in large numbers. The International Organization for Migration reported that about 230,000 had returned from Pakistan as of mid-November and projected that approximately 300,000 undocumented Afghans would return by the end of 2016. Approximately 391,000 undocumented Afghans returned from Iran during the same period; most of these returns resulted from deportation by Iranian authorities.

Internally Displaced Persons

Internal population movements increased, mainly triggered by increasing armed conflict. The United Nations estimated there were 1.2 million IDPs in the country. According to the UN Office for Coordination of Humanitarian Affairs, 486,000 new IDPs fled their homes from January to November. Most IDPs left insecure rural areas and small towns seeking relatively greater safety and government services in larger towns and cities in the same province. All 34 provinces hosted IDP populations.

Limited humanitarian access caused delays in identifying, assessing, and providing timely assistance to IDPs and led to estimates of the total number of IDPs that were significantly larger than official figures. IDPs continued to lack access to basic protection, including personal and physical security and shelter. Many IDPs, especially in households with a female head, faced difficulty obtaining basic services because they did not have identity documents. Many IDPs in urban areas reportedly faced discrimination, lacked adequate sanitation and other basic services, and lived in constant risk of eviction from illegally occupied displacement sites, according to the Internal Displacement Monitoring Center. Women in IDP camps reported high levels of domestic violence. Limited opportunities to earn a livelihood following the initial displacement often led to secondary displacement, making tracking of vulnerable persons difficult. Even IDPs who had access to local social services sometimes had less access than their non-IDP neighbors, due to distance from the services or other factors.

Protection of Refugees

<u>Access to Asylum</u>: Laws do not provide for granting asylum or refugee status, and the government has not established a system for providing protection to refugees from other countries. Nonetheless, the government worked closely with the international community to protect and respond to the needs of Pakistani refugees, including an estimated 100,000 refugees who remained in UNHCR camps in Khost and Paktika Provinces after being displaced in 2014 following Pakistani military operations against insurgents across the border.

Section 3. Freedom to Participate in the Political Process

The constitution provides citizens the opportunity to choose their government in free and fair periodic elections held by secret ballot and based on universal and equal suffrage. Citizens exercised this ability in the 2014 presidential and provincial elections and the 2010 parliamentary elections. The Taliban and political actors attempted to use violence to intimidate voters during the 2014 presidential elections, which were also marred by allegations of widespread fraud and corruption. Parliamentary elections are mandated by the constitution to be held every five years; however, the regularly scheduled elections were not held in 2015, as the government had yet to complete promised electoral reforms. As a result members of the Wolesi Jirga (lower house of parliament) remained in office past the June 2015 expiration of their five-year terms by virtue of a presidential decree. In November the government replaced the members of its main electoral bodies--the Independent Election Commission (IEC) and the Independent Electoral Complaints Commission--a necessary first step in completing the anticipated reforms and proposing a new electoral calendar.

Elections and Political Participation

<u>Recent Elections</u>: According to the IEC, more than 6.8 million voters cast votes in the first round of the April 2014 presidential election. Although security incidents occurred throughout the country, they reportedly had only a modest impact on turnout, and there were no mass-casualty events. Of the eight presidential candidates who competed in the first round, former foreign minister Abdullah Abdullah and former finance minister Ashraf Ghani Ahmadzai received the most votes, 45 percent and 31.6 percent, respectively. Neither achieved the majority necessary, and a runoff election between the two was held in June 2014.

Allegations of fraud led to a dispute over the accuracy of the preliminary results announced by the IEC following the June 2014 runoff. Those results showed Ghani leading with 56.4 percent, compared with Abdullah's 43.5 percent. Following a protracted standoff, the two candidates agreed to a 100 percent audit of the ballot boxes and committed to forming a National Unity Government, with the runner-up assuming a newly created chief executive officer (CEO) position in the government. According to media reporting of leaked IEC data, the audit invalidated more than 850,000 fraudulent ballots of an estimated eight million. The IEC completed the election audit and named Ghani the winner in September 2014. In accordance with the National Unity Government agreement, Ghani then created the CEO position by presidential decree and named Abdullah to the position. The audit results were released publicly in February.

<u>Political Parties and Political Participation</u>: Negative associations of past political activity with violent militia groups and the former communist regime, as well as allegations of persistent corruption and inefficiency among political elites, led many citizens to view political parties with suspicion. The Political Party Law granted parties the right to exist as formal institutions for the first time in the country's history. The law requires parties to have at least 10,000 members from the country's 34 provinces.

Parties were not always able to conduct activities throughout the country; in some regions antigovernment violence reduced security. As of November, 57 political parties were registered with the Ministry of Justice, and no party was deregistered during the year. According to the ministry, a deregistered party could meet and continue "informal" political activities, but candidates for political office could not run for office under the party's name until it met the registration criteria.

Provincial party members continued to assert the ministry's monitoring process was inconsistent. Some parties reported regular interactions with ministry officials and others had none at all. Political parties played a greater role in the 2014 presidential elections than in previous elections, and the organization, networks, and public support of the parties that supported Abdullah and Ghani contributed to their success as presidential candidates.

<u>Participation of Women and Minorities</u>: The constitution specifies a minimum number of seats for women and minorities in the two houses of parliament. For the Wolesi Jirga (lower house), the constitution mandates that at least two women shall be elected from each province (for a total of 68). In 2010 voters elected 69 women to the Wolesi Jirga. In the Meshrano Jirga (upper house), the constitution empowers the president to appoint one-third of the members. One-half of the presidential appointees must be women. Ten seats are also set aside in the Wolesi Jirga for members of the Kuchi minority (nomads). In the Meshrano Jirga, the president's appointees must include two Kuchis and two members with physical disabilities. In practice, one seat in the Meshrano Jirga is reserved for the appointment of a Sikh or Hindu representative, although this is not mandated by the constitution.

Traditional societal practices continued to limit women's participation in politics and activities outside the home and community, including the need to have a male escort or permission to work. These factors, in addition to an education and experience gap, likely continued to influence the central government's male-dominated composition. The 2013 electoral law reduced quotas for women on provincial councils from 25 percent to 20 percent and eliminated women's quotas entirely for district and village councils. Neither district nor village councils had been established by year's end.

As did their male counterparts, women active in government and politics continued to face threats and violence and were the targets of attacks by the Taliban and other insurgent groups. In July the director of women's affairs in Ghazni Province was attacked. She escaped unharmed, but another government employee was killed. Most female parliamentarians reportedly experienced some kind of threat or intimidation, and many believed the state could not or would not protect them.

No laws prevent minorities from participating in political life, although different ethnic groups complained they did not have equal access to local government jobs in provinces where they were in the minority. Individuals from the majority Pashtun ethnic group had more seats than any other ethnic group in both houses of parliament but did not have more than 50 percent of the seats. There was no evidence specific societal groups were excluded.

Section 4. Corruption and Lack of Transparency in Government

The law provides criminal penalties for corruption by officials. The government did not implement the law effectively or evenly, and there were reports officials frequently engaged in corrupt practices with impunity.

Reports indicated corruption remained endemic throughout society, and flows of money from the military, international donors, and the drug trade continued to exacerbate the problem. According to public opinion surveys, many citizens believed the government had not been effective in combating corruption. Corruption and uneven governance continued to play a significant role in allowing the Taliban to exert influence and control some areas in the southern, eastern, and some northern provinces, particularly in remote areas.

According to prisoners and local NGOs, corruption was widespread across the justice system, particularly in connection with the prosecution of criminal cases and in arranging release from prison. There were also reports that officials received unauthorized payments in exchange for reducing prison sentences, halting an investigation, or dismissing charges outright. The practice of filing criminal complaints in what would ordinarily be civil matters was commonly used to settle business disputes or extort money from wealthy international investors.

During the year there were reports of "land grabbing" by both private and public actors. The most common type occurred when businesses illegally obtained property deeds from corrupt officials and sold the deeds to unsuspecting "homeowners," who would then be caught up in criminal prosecutions. Other reports indicated government officials grabbed land without compensation to exchange it for contracts or political favors. Occasionally provincial governments illegally confiscated land without due process or compensation to build public facilities.

Corruption: In June the president signed a decree establishing an independent Anti-Corruption Justice Center with responsibility for prosecuting high-level corruption cases. With collaboration from the Supreme Court, AGO, and Major Crimes Task Force, prosecutors and primary and appellate court judges were assigned to the court, and work began on a permanent facility at Camp Heath. The anticorruption center began trying its first cases on November 12 in temporary facilities. In its first case, a senior-level AGO Military Department prosecutor was convicted for accepting a 43,500 Afghani ($750) bribe and sentenced to 2.5 years in prison and a 43,500 Afghani ($750) fine. In a second case, the deputy branch manager of Azizi Bank in Kandahar was convicted on four separate counts of embezzlement and forgery totaling 8.8 million Afghanis ($152,000), and he was sentenced to imprisonment for 10 years and four months. International media and observers attended the proceedings and reported the trials were procedurally fair, orderly, and professional.

Provincial police sometimes engaged in corruption at police checkpoints and from the narcotics industry. ANP officers reportedly paid higher-level Ministry of Interior officials for their positions and promotions. The justice system rarely pursued corruption cases, especially if they involved police. The ministry continued to be affected by allegations of widespread corruption, poor performance, and abuse of power by officers.

In addition to impunity, low salaries in the public sector and security forces exacerbated corruption by officials. The international community worked with the national and provincial governance structures to address the problem of low salaries, but implementation of grade reform remained slow.

Police reportedly demanded bribes from civilians to gain release from prison or avoid arrest. Citizens bribed corrections and detention officials to obtain release of prisoners who were not discharged at the end of their sentences.

Governors with reported involvement in corruption, the drug trade, or records of human rights violations reportedly continued to receive executive appointments and served with relative impunity.

Financial Disclosure: The High Office of Oversight is responsible for collecting information from senior government officials on all sources and levels of personal income. The office verifies and publishes online and in mass media the personal asset declarations of the most senior officials when they assume office and when they leave. While collection and publication occurred, some officials failed to submit the required reports, and there was only limited progress on the verification of such declarations by independent experts. The absence of legal penalties for omissions or misrepresentations tended to undermine this key tool for identifying wrongdoing.

<u>Public Access to Information</u>: The constitution and law provide citizens the right to access government information, except when access might violate the rights of others. Access to information from official sources continued to be limited due to a lack of clarity regarding citizens' rights and a lack of transparency among government institutions. NGOs and human rights organizations said the 2014 law on access to information had not yet been fully implemented, and some government officials reportedly failed to disclose information of public interest in an adequate manner. Observers noted concern about some provisions of the law authorities can use to withhold information for national security reasons. NGOs continued to point out that the lack of clear definitions for terms such as national security and national interest could seriously affect and limit access to information. On October 16, President Ghani issued a decree asking government officials not to delay access to information to media and to categorize information properly.

Section 5. Governmental Attitude Regarding International and Nongovernmental Investigation of Alleged Violations of Human Rights

Domestic and international human rights groups generally operated without government restriction, investigating and publishing their findings on human rights cases. While government officials were somewhat cooperative and responsive to their views, there were cases in which government officials intimidated human rights groups. Human rights activists continued to express concern that war criminals and human rights abusers remained in positions of power within the government.

<u>Government Human Rights Bodies</u>: The constitutionally mandated AIHRC continued to address human rights problems, but it received minimal government funding and relied almost exclusively on international donor funds.

Three Wolesi Jirga committees deal with human rights: the Gender, Civil Society, and Human Rights Committee; the Counternarcotics, Intoxicating Items, and Ethical Abuse Committee; and the Judicial, Administrative Reform, and Anticorruption Committee. In the Meshrano Jirga, the Committee for Gender and Civil Society addresses human rights concerns.

Section 6. Discrimination, Societal Abuses, and Trafficking in Persons

Women

<u>Rape and Domestic Violence</u>: The EVAW law criminalizes violence against women, including rape, battery, or beating; forced marriage; humiliation; intimidation; and deprivation of inheritance, although its implementation remained limited. The law provides for a sentence of 16 to 20 years' imprisonment for rape. If the act results in the death of the victim, the law provides for a death sentence for the perpetrator. The law provides for imprisonment of up to seven years for the "violation of chastity of a woman…that does not result in adultery (such as sexual touching)." Under the law, rape does not include spousal rape. The law was not widely understood, and some in the public and the religious communities deemed the law un-Islamic. Many authorities lacked the political will to implement the law and failed to enforce it fully.

The AIHRC reported 2,621 cases of violence against women from January through August, including nine killings, 79 cases of sexual violence, 34 sexual harassment cases, 733 beatings, and 44 forced engagements or marriages. Because of the security situation in the country, large numbers of violent crimes committed against women were unreported. In addition to AIHRC's report, the Ministry of Women's Affairs also reported 1,465 cases of violence against women within the first six months of the year, with Ghor, Baghlan, Badakshan, Nargarhar, Takhar, and Balkh Provinces showing the highest numbers.

The AGO operated 33 EVAW prosecution units in 33 provinces. In March the AGO held its second national meeting of EVAW prosecutors to facilitate communication between different provincial EVAW units and identify common issues. According to a January report by the Research Institute for Women Peace and Security, a domestic NGO, and the Chr. Michelsen Institute, of 2,958 cases registered with EVAW units in eight provinces studied, 792 or 27 percent resulted in indictments, and of these, 59 percent led to convictions. Among indicted cases, the conviction rate was highest for rape, with 73 percent of indictments leading to a conviction (41 percent of all registered rape cases resulted in convictions).

From March 2014 to March 2015, the government reported 4,541 registered cases of violence against women, with 3,038 registered under the EVAW law. The Ministry of Women's Affairs, Ministry of Interior, and AGO also registered 1,179 cases of divorce, separation, annulment of engagements, alimony, and child custody, which may or may not have stemmed from domestic violence, bringing the total number of registered cases to 5,720.

Pajhwork News released a report on the role of mediation outside the formal justice system in cases of violence against women. Because mediation takes place at the community level, the male-driven process restricted the reporting of violence against women cases. The same report showed a compilation of data of more than 21,000 of cases of violence against women over the last six years alone. Nearly 70 percent of the cases were registered with the Ministry of Women's Affairs and the police, but only an estimated 5 percent made it to the courts.

Prosecutors and judges in some remote provinces were unaware of the EVAW law, and others were subject to community pressure to release defendants due to familial loyalties, threat of harm, or bribes. Reports indicated men accused of rape often claimed the victim agreed to consensual sex, leading to zina charges against the victim, or perpetrators made false claims of marriage to the victim.

Rapes were difficult to document due to social stigma. Male victims seldom came forward due to fear of retribution or additional exploitation by authorities, but peer sexual abuse was reportedly common. Female victims faced stringent societal reprisal, ranging from being deemed unfit for marriage to being imprisoned for sexual conduct outside of marriage, or became victims of extrajudicial killing.

According to the 2016 Asia Foundation's *Annual Survey of the Afghan People*, only 23.8 percent of women surveyed knew of an organization, institution, or authority in their area where women could go to have their problems resolved. Forced virginity testing remains legal, and police, prosecutors, and judges frequently ordered virginity tests in cases where women or girls were accused of "moral crimes" such as zina. Women who sought assistance in cases of rape often became subjects of virginity tests and in some instances had their cases converted into adultery cases. According to a September 2015 AIHRC report on forced gynecological exams, 48 of 53 female prisoners interviewed had been subjected to virginity tests, and of these, 20 said they had been tested more than once. The AIHRC publicly condemned virginity testing, citing that the practice had no scientific basis and that performing medical tests without the patient's consent is a violation of the right to freedom and human dignity. Interpretations of sharia also impeded successful prosecution of rape cases.

In February media reported a group of armed kidnappers in Kapisa Province took a 10-year-old from her family's home and married her to one of the group leaders' son, a 30-year-old man. In July media reported that family members of a 15-year-old girl in Baghlan Province killed her and a 17-year-old male after accusing them of committing zina. In April a group of armed men gang-raped an 18-year-old in her home in Balkh Province.

The penal code criminalizes assault, and courts convicted domestic abusers under this provision, as well as the beating provision in the EVAW law. According to NGO reports, hundreds of thousands of women continued to suffer abuse at the hands of their husbands, fathers, brothers, in-laws, armed individuals, parallel legal systems, and institutions of state, such as the police and justice systems.

Police response to domestic violence was limited, in part due to low reporting, sympathy toward perpetrators, and limited protection for victims. Some police and judicial officials were unaware or unconvinced that rape was a serious criminal offense, and investigating rape cases was generally not a priority. Even in instances in which justice officials took rape seriously, some cases reportedly did not proceed due to bribery, family or tribal pressure, or other interference during the process. The AIHRC's 2013 report on rape and honor killing asserted that one-third of cases on rape and honor killings were addressed in accordance with the law. In its study the AIHRC found that 35 percent of rape and honors killings were not appropriately prosecuted. The AIHRC and NGOs contended that due to societal acceptance of the practice, most cases were unreported and never reached prosecutors.

According to the AIHRC, more than 2,579 cases of violence against women were reported between March and September 2015. The AIHRC noted that the majority of reports concerned verbal and psychological violence and noted an increase in the number of reported cases from the same period the previous year. The Ministry of Women's Affairs reported that up to 600 cases of violence against women were registered in the first three months of the year, the majority of which involved physical violence. Accurate statistics on the extent of violence against women, however, were difficult to obtain. The most recent research done on the prevalence of violence against women (as opposed to reported cases) was conducted by Global Rights and published in 2008. According to that report, 87 percent of women had experienced some form of physical, sexual, or psychological violence in their lives, and 62 percent had experienced more than one type of violence.

Most women did not seek legal assistance for domestic or sexual abuse because they did not know their rights or because they feared prosecution or return to their family or the perpetrator. Women sometimes practiced self-immolation, and the Ministry of Women's Affairs reported there continued to be cases of suicide as a result of domestic violence. Women continued to turn to NGO-run women's protection centers (women's shelters) and associated family guidance centers for assistance, and according to UNAMA's April 2015 report on women's access to justice, victims particularly valued the physical protection afforded by these centers, which often represented the only safe refuge for women. According to NGOs that ran women's protection centers countrywide, police continued to make up the most significant source of referrals, likely reflecting improved ANP training and awareness.

Space at the 28 women's protection centers across the country was sometimes insufficient, particularly in major urban centers, and shelters remained concentrated in the western, northern, and central regions of the country. Women who could not be reunited with their families or who were unmarried were generally compelled to remain in protection centers indefinitely, because "unaccompanied" women were not commonly accepted in society. The difficulty of finding durable solutions for women compelled to stay in protection centers was compounded by societal attitudes toward the shelters as centers of prostitution, the belief that "running away from home" was a serious violation of social mores, and the continued victimization of women who were raped but perceived by society as adulterers.

Women in need of protection who could not find it often ended up in prison, either due to a lack of a protection center in their province or district, or based on local interpretation of "running away" as a moral crime. Adultery, fornication, and kidnapping are crimes under the law. Women often were convicted of those crimes in situations of abuse, rape, or forced marriage, or on the basis of invalid evidence, including virginity tests. Running away is not a crime under the law, and both the Supreme Court and AGO issued directives to this effect, but women and girls continued to be detained for running away from home or "attempted zina." As of November 30, approximately 51 percent of female prisoners were incarcerated for moral crimes, according to GDPDC records.

The Ministry of Women's Affairs, as well as nongovernmental entities, sometimes arranged marriages for women who could not return to their families.

Police units charged with addressing violence against women, children, and families, included female officers. Although trained to help victims of domestic violence, the officers were hindered by instructions to wait for victims to take the initiative and reach out to them.

<u>Other Harmful Traditional Practices</u>: The EVAW law criminalizes forced, underage, and "baad" marriages (the practice of settling disputes in which the culprit's family trades a girl to the victim's family to settle a dispute) and

interference with a woman's right to choose her spouse. According to the United Nations and Human Rights Watch, an estimated 70 percent of marriages were forced. Despite laws banning the practice, many brides continued to be younger than the legal marriage age of 16 (or 15 with a guardian's and a court's approval). Some local media reported an increase in child marriages during the year, although it was unclear whether this reflected an actual increase in the practice or rather an increase in reports. A 2014 AIHRC survey found more than 7 percent of respondents reported their daughters were married before the age of 16. Very few marriages were legally registered with the state, leaving forced marriages outside of legal control.

Violence against women is also often a driving factor in cases of suicide and self-immolation. Under the penal code, a man convicted of honor killing after finding his wife committing adultery cannot be sentenced to more than two years' imprisonment. Honor killings continued, although accurate statistics were difficult to obtain. In July a 14-year-old pregnant girl in Ghor Province died in a local hospital after being burned alive in an honor killing by her husband and his family. When the girl's father reported the harassment and violence his daughter had suffered to the police, local authorities dismissed him and suggested he should settle the differences with the girl's in-laws. There were reports of summary justice by the Taliban and other antigovernment elements that resulted in extrajudicial executions. In June a woman in Ghor Province was abducted and shot after cancelling her engagement, and in July the Taliban publicly executed a 19-year-old woman in Sar-e-Pul Province for running away from home after a domestic dispute. UNAMA reported that the Taliban lashed a woman in the Sha Joy district of Zabul Province, citing adultery.

Sexual Harassment: The EVAW law criminalizes harassment and persecution of women but does not define these terms. A Regulation on Prohibition of Women's Sexual Harassment entered into effect in October 2015, when it was published in the official gazette. The regulation, which was adopted pursuant to the EVAW law, defines harassment against women and establishes and identifies mechanisms for complaint and redress. Women who walked outside alone or who worked outside the home often experienced abuse or harassment, including groping, or they were followed on the streets in urban areas. Women who took on public roles that challenged gender stereotypes (such as lawmakers, political leaders, NGO leaders, police officers, and news broadcasters) continued to be intimidated by conservative elements and received death threats directed at them or their families. NGOs reported violence, including killings, against women working in the public and nonprofit sectors and initiated awareness-raising campaigns to mobilize groups against harassment. Female members of the ANP reported harassment by their male counterparts, and there were reports that female ANP members and their families experienced intimidation and discrimination within their communities. In May a group of female social activists launched a website to help women register and report incidents of violence and seek advice on how to resolve their issues.

Reproductive Rights: Women generally exercised little decision-making authority regarding marriage, the timing, and number of pregnancies, birthing practices, and child education. Couples were free from government discrimination, coercion, and violence to decide the number, spacing, and timing of their children, although family and community pressures to reproduce, the high prevalence of child and early marriages, and lack of accurate biological knowledge limited their ability to do so. Women could expect to bear on average 5.1 children in their lifetimes. Oral contraceptives, intrauterine devices, injectable contraceptives, and condoms were available commercially and were provided at no cost in public health facilities and at subsidized rates in private health facilities and through community health workers. The UN Population Fund estimated that 23 percent of women of reproductive age used a modern method of contraception. Between January and August, the AIHRC registered eight cases of forced abortion from women and girls.

According to the World Health Organization's, UN's, and World Bank's *Trends in Maternal Mortality Report: 1990-2013*, the maternal mortality rate in 2013 was 400 deaths per 100,000 live births. This represented a two-thirds reduction in maternal mortality since 1995. Early marriage and pregnancy put girls at greater risk for premature labor, complications during delivery, and death in childbirth. Postpartum hemorrhage and obstructed labor were key causes of maternal mortality. Only 34 percent of births were attended by a skilled health practitioner, and only 21 percent of girls and women between the ages of 15 and 49 used a modern form of contraception.

Discrimination: Women who reported cases of abuse or who sought legal redress for other matters reported they experienced discrimination within the judicial system. Some observers, including female judges, asserted that discrimination was a result of faulty implementation of law and cultural nuances, rather than the law itself. A woman's limited access to money and other resources to pay fines (or bribes) and the social requirement for women to have a male guardian affected their access to and participation in the justice system. Local practices were discriminatory against women in some areas, particularly in parts of the country where courts were not functional or knowledge of the law was minimal. Judges in some remote districts acknowledged wide influence by tribal authorities in preempting cases from the formal justice system. In August 2015 a man beheaded his wife in Baghlan Province after she sought a divorce from a local court.

In the informal system, elders relied on interpretations of sharia and tribal customs, which generally discriminated against women. Many women reported limited access to justice in male-dominated tribal shuras, where proceedings focused on reconciliation with the community and family rather than the rights of the individual. Women in some villages were not allowed any access to dispute resolution mechanisms. Lack of awareness of their legal rights and illiteracy also limited women's ability to access justice. Women's advocacy groups reported in some cases that the government intervened informally with local courts to encourage them to interpret laws in ways favorable to women. Many cases in remote districts, however, reportedly were resolved according to the local police officer's or prosecutor's discretion or interpretation of the law. When legal authorities were aware of the EVAW law and its implementation, women were in some cases able to get appropriate assistance. Prosecutors in some provinces, however, continued to be reluctant to use the EVAW law. Moreover, in cases in which prosecutors brought charges under the EVAW law, judges would sometimes replace those charges with others based on the penal code.

Police, prosecutors, and judges discriminated against women in criminal and civil legal proceedings stemming from violence and forced marriages. Enhanced availability of legal aid, including through female attorneys, provided some relief in formal justice system proceedings.

Cultural prohibitions limiting women's movement prevented many women from working outside the home and reduced their access to education, health care, police protection, and other social services. In December the head of the council of religious scholars (Ulema Council) in Takhar Province declared women were the "most shameful" persons. He was fired immediately after his statement.

The law provides for equal work without discrimination, but there are no provisions for equal pay for equal work. The EVAW law criminalizes interference with a woman's right to work. Women faced discrimination in access to employment and terms of occupation. Some educated urban women found substantive work, but many were relegated to menial tasks in the workplace, regardless of qualification. There were 2,834 female police officers as of September 2015, including those in training, constituting less than 2 percent of the total police force. While the government made efforts to recruit additional female police officers, cultural customs and discrimination rendered recruitment and retention difficult. Women in high-profile positions of government service continued to be subjected to threats and violence.

The Ministry of Women's Affairs and NGOs promoted women's rights and freedoms. According to the AIHRC, many women in the civil service did not meet the minimum qualification of a bachelor's degree imposed by the priority reform and restructuring system. The women's ministry, the primary government agency responsible for addressing gender policy and the needs of women, had offices in all provinces and established gender units in all ministries. Gender units at lower ranks, however, lacked major influence, and men typically dominated their leadership positions. Although the ministry's provincial offices assisted hundreds of women by providing legal and family counseling and referring women, they could not directly assist relevant organizations. The ministry and provincial line directorates suffered from a lack of capacity and resources.

Despite improvements in health over the past decade, the overall health of women and children remained poor, particularly among nomadic and rural populations and those in insecure areas. As with men, women's life expectancy was 64 years of age. Rural women suffered disproportionately from insufficient numbers of skilled health personnel, particularly female health workers.

Compared to men, women and children were disproportionately victims of preventable deaths due to communicable diseases. Although free health services were provided in public facilities, many households could not afford certain costs related to medicines or transportation to health-care facilities, and many women were not permitted to travel to health-care facilities on their own.

Children

Birth Registration: A citizen father transmits citizenship to his child. Birth in the country or to a citizen mother alone is not sufficient. Adoption is not legally recognized.

Education: Education is mandatory up to the lower secondary level (six years for primary school and three years for lower secondary), and the law provides for free education up to and including the college level. Many children, however, did not attend school.

According to UNICEF's April report on health care and education, 369 schools closed in 2015, and 139,000 children were out of school. Military operations and increased levels of violence impeded children's access to education. Use of school buildings by both ANDSF and militants also affected children's ability to attend school, especially for young girls. On June 4 and July 4, the Ministry of Education issued two directives asking security forces to stop using schools for military purposes.

In most regions boys and girls attended primary classes together but were separated for intermediate and secondary education. According to a statement by the Ministry of Education on December 18, of the country's nine million registered schoolchildren, 24 percent did not attend school. The ministry estimated 3.5 million schoolchildren, or 39 percent, were girls. Many students were not enrolled full-time or dropped out early.

According to the *Education for All 2015 National Review Report: Afghanistan*, in 2013 the gross enrollment rate for girls as a percentage of total enrollment was approximately 41 percent at the primary level, 36 percent at the lower secondary level, and 35 percent at the upper secondary level. According to the same report, the literacy rate for girls and women 15 to 24 years of age was 32 percent as of 2012.

The status of girls and women in education was a matter of grave concern. Key obstacles to girls' education included poverty, early and forced marriage, insecurity, lack of family support, lack of female teachers, and the long distance to school. Former president Karzai's 2012 Decree on Governance and Corruption addressed the lack of female teachers, particularly in conservative rural areas, by charging the Education Ministry with recruiting an additional 11,000 teachers and increasing the number of district-level teacher training support centers to provide training opportunities for female teachers. According to the ministry, there were 202,336 teachers in public schools, and 33 percent of them were women as of November. There were 20,337 teachers in private schools, and 52 percent were women.

Violent attacks on schoolchildren, particularly girls, also hindered access to education. Violence impeded access to education in various sections of the country, particularly in areas controlled by the Taliban. The Taliban and other extremists threatened and attacked school officials, teachers, and students, particularly girls, and burned both boys' and girls' schools. Between January and June, UNAMA documented 25 incidents of threat and intimidation targeting schools, students, or schools staff. According to reports submitted to UNAMA, on January 7, 15 masked men entered a girls' high school in Jowzjan Province and warned that female students over 12 must wear burqas. Following the threat, the school's principal imposed a requirement for all girls over 12 to wear burqas. On April 13, in an attack by Taliban forces in Laghman Province, Taliban insurgents attacked Besram high school near the provincial capital of Mehtar Lam City, leaving two students dead and three students injured when stray bullets hit the school. On April 20, a headmaster in Khwaja Bahauddin district of Takhar Province was killed by a stray bullet in front of his students.

Insecurity, conservative attitudes, and poverty denied education to millions of school-age children, mainly in the southern and southeastern provinces. A representative from the Ministry of Education estimated in November that 140,000 schoolchildren in insecure areas did not have access to education. There were also reports of abduction and molestation. The lack of community-based, nearby schools was another factor inhibiting school attendance.

Child Abuse: NGOs reported increased numbers of child abuse victims during the year, and the problem remained endemic throughout the country. Such abuse included general neglect, physical abuse, sexual abuse, abandonment, and confined forced labor to pay off family debts. Police reportedly beat and sexually abused children; for instance, Agence France-Presse reported a case of a 13-year-old boy kidnapped by a police commander in southern Helmand. NGOs reported a predominantly punitive and retributive approach to juvenile justice throughout the country. Although it is against the law, corporal punishment in schools, rehabilitation centers, and other public institutions remained common.

Sexual abuse of children was pervasive. NGOs noted girls were more frequently abused by extended family members, while boys were more frequently abused by men outside their families. In November a five-year-old girl in Baghlan Province was allegedly raped by relatives of her older sister's fiance after her sister ran off with another man. There were reports religious figures sexually abused both boys and girls. NGOs noted families often were complicit, allowing local strongmen to abuse their children in exchange for status or money. The Ministry of Interior tracked cases of rape, but most NGOs and observers estimated the official numbers significantly underreported the phenomenon. Many perpetrators of child sexual abuse were not arrested, and there were reports security officials and those connected to the ANP raped children with impunity. The practice continued of bacha baazi (dancing boys), which involved powerful or wealthy local figures and businessmen sexually abusing young boys trained to dance in female clothes. Reports of the practice increased since 2001.

There were multiple reports and press articles on the rape of young boys who were forcibly kept as bachas. After a June 15 article the Agence France-Presse published on Taliban forces using bacha baazi to infiltrate and carry out attacks against Afghan security forces, President Ghani ordered an investigation of sexual abuse cases in the security forces. The President's Office stated that anyone, regardless of rank, found guilty of engaging in bacha baazi would be prosecuted. The government did not release a report on the investigation. At year's end no known prosecutions of perpetrators in the security forces had taken place.

A September 2015 article in the *New York Times* documented the practice of bacha baazi by progovernment forces in Kunduz Province. Following the report, the Ministries of Interior and Defense and the President's Office issued statements condemning the practice. The president also ordered the creation of a working committee, including the AIHRC, Interior Ministry, and AGO, to investigate and monitor cases of abuse and create a mechanism to prevent and prosecute perpetrators. There were no reports on the progress of the committee.

The government took few other steps to discourage the abuse of boys or to prosecute or punish those involved. On December 12, President Ghani signed a new trafficking-in-persons law, which includes legal provisions criminalizing behaviors associated with the sexual exploitation of children. In 2014 the AIHRC released its national inquiry on bacha baazi. The report asserted bacha baazi was a form of trafficking already criminalized and called on the government to enforce the law actively. It attributed the root causes of the practice to lack of rule of law, corruption, gaps in the law, poverty, insecurity, and the existence of armed insurgent groups. The report noted the serious psychological and physical harm victims faced and called on the government to provide protective services to victims.

Early and Forced Marriage: Despite a law setting the legal minimum age for marriage at 16 (15 with the consent of a parent or guardian and the court) for girls and 18 for boys, international and local observers continued to report widespread early marriage. A 2014 survey by the Ministry of Public Health showed 53 percent of all women ages 25-49 married by age 18 and 21 percent by age 15. According to the Central Statistics Organization of Afghanistan, 17 percent of girls ages 15 to 19 were married. During the EVAW law debate, conservative politicians publicly stated it was un-Islamic to ban the marriage of girls younger than 16. Under the

EVAW law, those who arrange forced or underage marriages may be sentenced to imprisonment for not less than two years, but implementation of the law was limited. The Law on Marriage states marriage of a minor may be conducted with a guardian's consent.

By law a marriage contract requires verification that the bride is 16 years of age (or 15 with the permission of her parents or a court), but only a small fraction of the population had birth certificates. Following custom, some poor families pledged their daughters to marry in exchange for "bride money," although the practice is illegal. According to local NGOs, some girls as young as six or seven were promised in marriage, with the understanding the actual marriage would be delayed until the child reached puberty. Reports indicated, however, that this delay was rarely observed and that young girls were sexually violated by the groom or by older men in the family, particularly if the groom was also a child. Media reports also noted the "opium bride" phenomenon, in which farming families married off their daughters to settle debts to opium traffickers.

There were multiple media reports of girls given in baad or sold. In July an elderly mullah was arrested in Ghor Province for marrying a six-year-old girl. The girl's father was also arrested after the mullah claimed that he was given the girl as a religious offering in exchange for prayers and a few goods. In August an 18-year-old woman in Badghis Province was beheaded by her husband's family after asking for a divorce. The victim was only three years old when her father arranged her engagement to a local boy.

Other Harmful Traditional Practices: Girls under age 18 continued to be at risk for honor killings for perceived sexual relations outside of marriage, running away, not accepting a forced marriage, or being a victim of sexual assault. In July 2015 media reported family members of a 15-year-old girl in Baghlan Province shot and killed her and a 17-year-old boy after the two returned home following an elopement.

Sexual Exploitation of Children: Although pornography is a crime, child pornography is not specifically identified under the law. Exploiting a child for sexual purposes, often associated with bacha baazi, was widespread, although some aspects of this practice are separate crimes under the penal code.

Child Soldiers: In February the Law on Prohibition of Children's Recruitment in the Military became effective. There were reports the ANDSF and progovernment militias used children for specific purposes in a limited number of cases, and the

Taliban and other antigovernment elements recruited children for military purposes (see section 1.g.). Media reported that local progovernment commanders recruited children under 16 years of age. These children participated in military operations against the Taliban in the Baharak district of Badakhshan. UNAMA documented 15 incidents of recruitment and use of children by pro- and antigovernment groups. Taliban trained at least three boys, including a nine-year-old boy with mental disability, for suicide attacks in Kandahar and Nangarhar.

Displaced Children: The Ministry of Labor, Social Affairs, Martyrs, and Disabled and the AIHRC continued to estimate the number of street children in the country at six million, but the National Census Directorate had not conducted a recent survey. Street children had little or no access to government services, although several NGOs provided access to basic needs, such as shelter and food.

Institutionalized Children: Living conditions for children in orphanages were poor. The social affairs ministry oversaw 84 Child Protection Action Network centers and 78 residential orphanages, which were designed to provide vocational training to children from destitute families. Of these, 30 were privately funded orphanages and 48 were government-funded centers operated by NGOs by agreement with the ministry. NGOs reported up to 80 percent of children between ages four and 18 years in the orphanages were not orphans but came from families that could not provide food, shelter, or schooling. Children in orphanages reported mental, physical, and sexual abuse and occasionally were subjected to trafficking. They did not have regular access to running water, heating in winter, indoor plumbing, health services, recreational facilities, or education.

International Child Abductions: The country is not a party to the 1980 Hague Convention on the Civil Aspects of International Child Abduction. See the Department of State's *Annual Report on International Parental Child Abduction* at travel.state.gov/content/childabduction/en/legal/compliance.html.

Anti-Semitism

There was no Jewish community in the country, and there were no reports of anti-Semitic acts.

Trafficking in Persons

See the Department of State's *Trafficking in Persons Report* at www.state.gov/j/tip/rls/tiprpt/.

Persons with Disabilities

The constitution prohibits any kind of discrimination against citizens and requires the state to assist persons with disabilities and to protect their rights, including the rights to health care and financial protection. The constitution also requires the state to adopt measures to reintegrate and provide for the active participation in society of persons with disabilities. The Law on the Rights and Benefits of Disabled Persons provides for equal rights to, and the active participation of, such persons in society. The Ministry of Labor, Social Affairs, Martyrs, and Disabled continued to implement a five-year national action plan through a memorandum of understanding with the Ministry of Information and Culture and the Ministry of Education to implement public awareness programs on the rights of persons with disabilities through national media and to provide scholarships for students with disabilities. There were reports the information ministry was not cooperative regarding implementation of the memorandum of understanding.

During the year there were approximately 80,000 persons with disabilities registered with the ministry who received financial support from the government. Persons with 30 to 60 percent disability received an annual payment of 26,100 Afghanis ($450), and persons with more than 60 percent disability received a total of 52,200 Afghanis ($900) annually.

Disability rights activists reported that corruption prevented some persons with disabilities from receiving benefits. There were reports that government officials redirected scholarship funds for persons with disabilities to friends or family through fraud and identity theft. NGOs and government officials also reported that associations of persons with disabilities attempted to intimidate ministry employees in an effort to secure benefits such as apartments.

Lack of security remained a challenge for disability programs. Insecurity in remote areas, where a disproportionate number of persons with disabilities lived, precluded delivery of assistance in some cases. The majority of buildings remained inaccessible to persons with disabilities, prohibiting many from benefitting from education, health care, and other services.

Persons with disabilities faced barriers such as limited access to educational opportunities, inability to access government buildings, lack of economic opportunities, and social exclusion. NGOs reported persons with disabilities faced difficulties accessing the majority of public buildings, including government ministries, health clinics, and hospitals. Society and even their own families mistreated persons with disabilities, since there was a common perception persons had disabilities because they or their parents had "offended God."

In the Meshrano Jirga, authorities reserved two of the presidentially appointed seats for persons with disabilities.

National/Racial/Ethnic Minorities

Ethnic tensions between various groups continued to result in conflict and killings.

Societal discrimination against Shia Hazaras continued along class, race, and religious lines in the form of extortion of money through illegal taxation, forced recruitment and forced labor, physical abuse, and detention. According to NGOs, the government frequently assigned Hazara ANP officers to symbolic positions with little authority within the Ministry of Interior. NGOs also reported Hazara ANSF officers were more likely than non-Hazara officers to be posted to insecure areas of the country.

Multiple kidnappings of Hazara were reported in several provinces, including Ghazni, Zabul, and Baghlan. The abductors reportedly shot, beheaded, ransomed, or released the kidnapping victims. In February 2015 unidentified gunmen abducted 31 Hazara men from a bus in Zabul Province. The abductors released 19 of the men in May and eight others in November. Four of the hostages remained unaccounted for at year's end.

Sikhs and Hindus faced discrimination, reporting unequal access to government jobs and harassment in school, as well as verbal and physical abuse in public places. According to the Sikh and Hindu Council of Afghanistan, there were approximately 900 members of the Sikh and Hindu community in the country.

Acts of Violence, Discrimination, and Other Abuses Based on Sexual Orientation and Gender Identity

The law criminalizes consensual same-sex sexual conduct, and there were reports that harassment, violence, and detentions by police continued. NGOs reported police arrested, detained, robbed, and raped gay men. The law does not prohibit discrimination or harassment based on sexual orientation or gender identity.

Homosexuality was widely seen as taboo and indecent. Members of the lesbian, gay, bisexual, transgender, and intersex (LGBTI) community did not have access to certain health services and could be fired from their jobs because of their sexual orientation. Organizations devoted to protecting the freedom of LGBTI persons remained underground because they could not be legally registered. Members of the LGBTI community reported they continued to face discrimination, assault, rape, and arrest.

HIV and AIDS Social Stigma

There were no confirmed reports of discrimination or violence against persons with HIV/AIDS, but there was reportedly serious societal stigma against persons with AIDS.

Section 7. Worker Rights

a. Freedom of Association and the Right to Collective Bargaining

The law provides for the right of workers to join and form independent unions and to conduct legal strikes and bargain collectively, and the government generally respected these rights, although it lacked enforcement tools. The law, however, provides no definition of a union or its relationship with employers and members, nor does it establish a legal method for union registration or penalties for violations. The law does not prohibit antiunion discrimination or provide for reinstatement of workers fired for union activity. Other than protecting the right to participate in a union, the law provides no other legal protection for union workers or workers seeking to unionize.

Although the law identifies the Ministry of Labor, Social Affairs, Martyrs, and Disabled's Labor High Council as the highest decision-making body on labor-related issues, the lack of implementing regulations prevented the council from performing its function. There was an inspection office within the ministry, but inspectors could only advise and make suggestions. As a result the application of labor law remained limited because of a lack of central enforcement authority, implementing regulations that describe procedures and penalties for violations, funding, personnel, and political will.

The government allowed several unions to operate without interference or political influence. Freedom of association and the right to bargain collectively were generally respected, but most workers were not aware of these rights. This was particularly true of workers in rural areas or the agricultural sector, who had not formed unions. In urban areas the majority of workers participated in the informal sector as day laborers in construction, where there were neither unions nor collective bargaining.

b. Prohibition of Forced or Compulsory Labor

The law prohibits all forms of forced or compulsory labor. The law prescribes penalties, including a "maximum term" of imprisonment for forced labor (between eight and 15 years). Article 515 of the penal code also could be interpreted to criminalize a "foreign party's" coercive labor practices through fraud or deceit, with a penalty of five to 15 years' imprisonment.

Government enforcement of the law was ineffective; resources, inspections, and remediation were inadequate; and the government made minimal efforts to prevent and eliminate forced labor. Penalties were insufficient to deter violations.

Forced labor occurred. Men, women, and children were forced into poppy cultivation, domestic work, carpet weaving, brick kiln work, organized begging, and drug trafficking. NGO reports documented the practice of bonded labor, whereby customs allow families to force men, women, and children to work as a means to pay off debt or to settle grievances. The debt can continue from generation to generation, with children forced to work to pay off their parents' debt (see section 7.c.). Labor violations against migrant workers were common, especially the widespread practice of bonded labor in brick kiln facilities.

Also see the Department of State's *Trafficking in Persons Report* at www.state.gov/j/tip/rls/tiprpt/.

c. Prohibition of Child Labor and Minimum Age for Employment

The labor law sets the minimum age for employment at 18 but permits 14-year-olds to work as apprentices, allows children who are 15 and older to do "light work," and permits children 16 and 17 to work up to 35 hours per week. Children under age 14 are prohibited from working under any circumstances. The law prohibits the employment of children in work likely to threaten their health or cause disability, including mining, begging, and garbage collection; work in blast furnaces, waste-processing plants, and large slaughterhouses; work with hospital waste; drug-related work; security guard services; and work related to war.

The government lacked a specific policy on implementing the law's provisions on child labor. Poor institutional capacity was a serious impediment to effective enforcement of the labor law. Deficiencies included inadequate resources, inspections, remediation, and penalties for violations, and the government made minimal efforts to prevent child labor or remove children from exploitative labor conditions. Reports estimated that fewer than 10 percent of children had formal birth registrations, which further limited authorities' already weak capacity to enforce laws on the minimum age of employment.

Child labor remained a pervasive problem. The Ministry of Labor declined to estimate the number of working children, citing a lack of data and deficiencies in birth registrations.

Child laborers worked as domestic servants, street vendors, peddlers, and shopkeepers, and in carpet weaving, brick making, the coal industry, and poppy harvesting. Children were also heavily engaged in the worst forms of child labor in agriculture, mining (especially family-owned gem mines), commercial sexual exploitation (see section 6, Children), transnational drug smuggling, and organized begging rings. Some forms of child labor exposed children to land mines. Children faced numerous health and safety risks at work, and there were reports children were exposed to sexual abuse by adult workers. There were reports of recruitment of juveniles by the ANDSF during the year. Taliban forces pressed children to take part in hostile acts (see section 6, Children).

Also see the Department of Labor's *Findings on the Worst Forms of Child Labor* at travel.state.gov/content/childabduction/en/legal/compliance.html.

d. Discrimination with Respect to Employment and Occupation

The constitution prohibits discrimination and notes that citizens, both "man and woman," have equal rights and duties before the law. It expressly prohibits discrimination based on language. The constitution contains no specific provisions addressing discrimination based on race, color, sex, religion, political opinion, national origin or citizenship, social origin, disability, sexual orientation or gender identity, age, HIV-positive status, or other communicable diseases. The penal code prescribes a term of imprisonment of not more than two years for anyone convicted of spreading discrimination or factionalism.

Women continued to face discrimination and hardship in the workplace. Women made up only 7 percent of the workforce. According to the 2016 Asia Foundation survey, 74 percent of the population agreed that women should be allowed to work outside the home; nonetheless, only 9.4 percent of women in the survey said they were involved in any activity that involved making money. Many women faced pressure from relatives to stay at home and encountered hiring practices that favored men. Older and married women reported it was more difficult for them than for younger, single women to find jobs. Women who worked reported they encountered insults, sexual harassment, lack of transportation, and an absence of day-care facilities. Salary discrimination existed in the private sector. Female journalists, social workers, and police officers reported they were often threatened or abused.

Ethnic Hazaras, Sikhs, and Hindus were subjected to discrimination in hiring and work assignments, in addition to broader social discrimination (see section 6, National/Racial/Ethnic Minorities).

e. Acceptable Conditions of Work

The minimum wage for permanent government workers was 6,000 Afghanis ($103) per month. There was no minimum wage for permanent workers in the private sector; but the minimum wage for workers in the nonpermanent private sector was 5,500 Afghanis ($95) per month. According to the Central Statistics Organization, 36 percent of the population earned wages below the poverty line of 1,150 Afghanis ($20) per month.

The law defines the standard workweek for both public- and private-sector employees as 40 hours: eight hours per day with one hour for lunch and noon prayers. The labor law makes no mention of day workers in the informal sector, leaving them completely unprotected. There are no occupational health and safety regulations or officially adopted standards. The law, however, provides for reduced standard workweeks for youth, pregnant women, nursing mothers, and miners and workers in other occupations that present health risks. The law provides workers with the right to receive wages, annual vacation time in addition to national holidays, compensation for on-the-job injuries, overtime pay, health insurance for the employee and immediate family members, and other incidental allowances. The law prohibits compulsory work and stipulates that overtime work be subject to the agreement of the employee. The law prohibits women and minors (ages 15 to 18) from engaging in physically challenging work, work that is harmful to health, and night work. The law also requires employers to provide day care and nurseries for children.

The government did not effectively enforce these laws. The labor ministry had only 18 inspectors for 34 provinces, and the inspectors had no legal authority to enter premises or impose penalties for violations. Resources, inspections, remediation, and penalties for violations were inadequate and insufficient to deter violations.

Employers often chose not to comply with the law or preferred to hire workers informally. Most employees worked longer than 40 hours per week, were frequently underpaid, and worked in poor conditions, particularly in the informal sector. Workers were generally unaware of the full extent of their labor rights under the law. Although comprehensive data on workplace accidents were unavailable, there were several reports of poor and dangerous working conditions. Some industries, such as brick kiln facilities, continued to use debt bondage, making it difficult for workers to remove themselves from situations that endangered their health or safety.